FIND YOUR VOICE

FIND YOUR VOICE
Capturing the Power of Influence to Live a Greater Story

ISBN 978-1-63570-067-1

Published by Orange, a division of The reThink Group, Inc.
5870 Charlotte Lane, Suite 300
Cumming, GA 30040 U.S.A.

Other Orange products are available online and direct from the publisher.

Visit our website at www.OrangeBooks.com for more resources like these.

Author: Sam Collier
Foreword: Tedashii
Lead Editor: Mike Jeffries
Editing Team: Sarah Shelton, Steph Whitacre
Project Manager: Nate Brandt
Cover and Interior Design: Donna Cunningham
Printed in the United States of America

First Edition 2018
2 3 4 5 6 7 8 9 10 11

04/11/18

DEDICATION

*I dedicate this book to everyone that helped me
FIND MY VOICE: My adopted parents, my
twin sister Sara, my friends, and my mentors.*

*Thank you guys for pushing me, supporting
me, challenging me and most importantly,
loving me.*

ENDORSEMENTS

"Finding your voice is important. In fact, it is the route to both internal and external success. This book outlines key concepts and principles required in order to master the power of your voice and its influence."

Cappriccieo M. Scates, Ambassador, *United Nations Economic and Social Council*

"Sam is one of the most important emerging voices in Christian leadership today with a passion to help others win in life, and that's exactly what he's doing in *Find Your Voice.*"

Andre Henry, Managing Editor, *Relevant Magazine*

"Sam Collier's a bright young mind with an incredible insight into what it means to use influence to bring out the best in others. In *Find Your Voice*, he challenges readers to accelerate that influence in their own lives at three distinct levels. I'm proud to have Sam on our team and I think there's extraordinary potential for young people to find their voice by listening to his advice."

Reggie Joiner, CEO and Founder, *reThink/Orange*

"Find Your Voice provides practical steps to discovering your own voice in the noisy world around us. Anyone interested in becoming a leader should consider this book essential. Sam reveals, with clarity and honesty, how he found his voice to become a national thought leader."

Joseph Sojourner, *CEO of Opposite Entertainment, Speaker, Recording Artist*

"Occasionally you meet someone and realize, 'This person is special.' When I met Sam Collier, it was evident there was greatness in him. The reason? He had found his voice and he was living into who God had created him to be. Now, I'm excited Sam has written *Find Your Voice* so you, too, can unleash the greatness that is in you."

Randy Gravitt, *CEO of InteGREAT Leadership and co-author of UnSTUCK*

"Sam is like the older brother young leaders wish they had. He passionately shares his story with a candid down-to-earth-ness that makes timeless leadership principles accessible to young leaders. One thing rings

loud and clear in *Find Your Voice*. Sam has the biggest heart for the discouraged and overlooked student and young adult. With a genuine and compassionate tone, he takes the time to share both the triumphs and misadventures he encountered on his journey to influence."

Leslie Mack, *Life.Church Creative Media, Content Development*

FOREWORD

By Tedashii

To most, this may seem like just another book on personal development, but it is so much more. This is a manual, a roadmap for survivors, on how to navigate the congested highways of our thoughts and emotions to find the road we were meant to travel so we don't just survive, but thrive.

From the very start, you get the sincere heart behind this book and preparation for the journey to come. You can almost hear the excitement and passion in his voice as you read. This is why I am grateful for Sam Collier, and people like him, who would take the time to think though such a topic and have the courage to give it to us straight up with no fluff. To passionately help us understand that there are levels of influence, most of us for the first time. From the personal stories and family shortcomings, to the hope expressed by a longshot daring to dream, you get the full truth and nothing else.

This is a book about purpose, but this one is different. I can honestly say that this is not like all the other books you find out there on this subject. Sam presents his case in such a unique and refreshing way that I found myself reevaluating and applying some of these very principles in my own life. See, I grew up without my father and in an environment very similar to what Sam describes in this book. In my world, most people lacked the stability and reinforcement of their identity or true potential and that left most constantly asking "why am I here" and "what am I supposed to do" with no real outlet for answers. I asked these questions so much I would get on people's nerves, and I never got a concrete response. I wanted someone to point me in the right direction or just tell me what I was supposed to do.

This book is the beginning to finding some of the very answers you've been searching for. Sam uses his own voice to help us find ours. We're all on a quest for what we are meant to be and I believe this book is an excellent tool to do just that. This is a book of transparency and vulnerability. What was even more inspiring about this is the eyewitness account of everything being presented to us. As you read, you begin to see the literary layers within the pages landing at the foundation of someone who has the testimony to support the truth being presented to the reader. It's from that place of sincerity that you may also be called upon to be just as transparent about who you are and where you truly find yourself right now.

From the moment I first met Sam, I knew I was sitting with someone who truly wanted to help others succeed at this thing called life. And it is from that place of victory that Sam endeavors to help others reach the same heights and beyond. This is a work derived from the depths of his real life but arranged and presented in such a way that people from all walks can relate. It is apparent through his writings that Sam has done the work to understand himself and all of his potential, and he is burdened to help us do the same.

The one thing I asked myself after finishing the book was, "Have I found my voice? Have I taken the necessary steps to maximize my voice to become the leader I was meant to be?" I have the privilege to travel around the globe raising my voice to be a leader of influence and this book made me evaluate myself and ask if I can do more. The fear is I can but I have not and I would have to admit that. A self-centered view only robs me and those around me of the things I have been uniquely created to offer in the world.

Don't allow this work to go to waste by just going through the motions to have another book you can check off the list with no real fruit from your time. You matter and what you have to offer can potentially change the world. Even if your story wasn't meant to be or seems like it's almost over, your voice matters. So take every word of this book to heart and pursue finding your voice as if you've never been heard before, because chances are, you haven't.

Tedashii
Hip Hop Artist and Public Speaker

FIND YOUR VOICE

THE POWER OF INFLUENCE

WHAT DOES IT MEAN TO FIND YOUR VOICE?

Well, I think another way to ask that same question is: What does it mean to FIND PURPOSE? I think it's no secret that we were all born for a reason. We all have different talents, passions, and dreams. This is evidence of purpose. I believe you were put here on this earth to do something special ... Finding your voice is discovering how you're going to use those talents, passions, and dreams to do that special thing that will make the world (and your world) better.

Finding your voice begins with understanding how influence works.

WHY DID I WRITE THIS BOOK?

I wrote this book because I was set up to fail.

My life was over before it began. I wasn't supposed to be successful. I'm not really supposed to be living at all. You see, I wasn't born into the best circumstances. I didn't meet my biological parents until I was 25. Most of the men in my family are doing something illegal, in jail, or dead.

Yet, somehow, I'm here. *I won.*

How did I win? I FOUND MY VOICE.

I wrote this book to tell you about one of the most powerful forces ever created—a secret to success and overcoming the obstacles you face:

THE POWER OF INFLUENCE

Maybe you're a student who's thinking about what's next in life or maybe you're just launching your career, but aren't sure where to begin.

I want to show you what *real* influence looks like and teach you how to leverage it for yourself. We'll identify the top three areas in which influence should be leveraged… all in an effort to help you defy the odds, just like I have, so you can ultimately make a difference.

WHAT IS INFLUENCE?

Influence is leadership and leadership is influence. When you say, "Someone is influencing you," you're essentially saying, "Someone is leading you." Leadership can be intentional or unintentional. You may not even know you're being led. Or you may not even know you're leading someone else. Either way, it's leadership.

Think about it for a second. Say you want to be an Olympic gymnast. There are potentially two ways to do it.

One way: You could find a coach to train with for years before you go on to win the medal.

Or another way: Just hang out with Gabby Douglas (a lot), learn from her in passing, and become like her (or at least something close to it). As unrealistic as that sounds, situations like that happen all of the time. People become amazing just by hanging around amazing people.

Whether it's intentionally following a coach's leadership or someone hanging out with an Olympic medalist, the outcome is still the same: GREATNESS. The path isn't as important as the outcome.

That doesn't mean some methods aren't more effective than others. In the case of Olympic gymnastics, having a coach is way more effective than just hanging out near the high beam. However, both paths lead to the same place. Knowing when and how to make the most of your surroundings and connections is what this book is all about.

THIS IS THE POWER OF INFLUENCE.

Influence comes to us in more than one way. The question is: Can you see it happening? Will you recognize it in your own life? This, my friends, will determine what you get out of the influence and leadership in your life.

For centuries, we've seen unforeseen influences take down countries, celebrities, regimes, and powerful men and women. We've seen unforeseen influences kill people. That's because when you're unaware that someone or something is influencing you, it leaves you in a very dangerous position. But when you can see it, that's when you begin to access the power of influence in your life. Then you can begin to manage it. And when you can manage it, the game changes!

For the next couple moments, let me lead you down a path to a greater story. Let me help you FIND YOUR VOICE. To do this, we need to focus on three groups of people that have the ability to change your life right now.

Friends.
Leaders.
Followers.

FIND YOUR VOICE by choosing the right FRIENDS.

I've been in those same school assemblies as you have. I remember hearing business and community leaders, millionaires, role models, celebrities, mentors, and even teachers repeating this one simple truth: Show me your FRIENDS, and I'll show you your DESTINY. Show me your FRIENDS, and I'll show you your FUTURE.

Now, I'll be honest. The moment any adult said this to me when I was a kid, I completely erased it from my memory. It was like my dad trying to tell me what music to listen to. Why would I ever listen to him about something so important?

Needless to say, I was wrong. Of course, I didn't learn that until many years later, after making many of the mistakes that the mentors, the millionaires, my teachers, my parents, and other role models warned me about. The truth is they were right: Your friends may be the most important voices in your life. Their voices are louder and greater than anyone else's. Your friends really do determine your future.

Here's why: As humans, we hunger for acceptance. We want validation. We long for belonging. And our friends give us those things. Therefore, our friends have the power to influence our . . .

thoughts,
decisions,
and atmosphere.

And those things? Well, they determine our FUTURE. The thoughts we entertain, the actions we choose, and the atmosphere in which we do life are huge factors in determining the direction of our lives.
At the end of the day, our friends are one of the biggest parts of shaping those three areas. That's why it's so important to pay attention to who our friends are.

Still don't believe me? Let me give you some examples.

LET'S START WITH OUR THOUGHTS.

When I was younger, I had two friends who grew up down the street from one another. One became a very successful executive at Google, and the other was eventually locked up and sent to prison for many years. Let's just call them *"The Google Exec"* and *"The Lost One."*

When we were younger, we all had choices. And on my block, we were faced with two specific choices: *The Right Way* or *The Wrong Way.* Even though the choice was challenging sometimes, we still had the option to choose which path we were going to take. My friends and I were all eventually asked the same questions from the same group of guys who had already made the choice to go *the wrong way.*

"Y'all wanna smoke?"
"Y'all wanna get some money?"
Your answers to questions like those dictate not just your next steps, but ultimately the outcome of your life.

The Google Exec said no to both of those questions.
The Lost One said yes. Not just once, but over and over again.

We tried to tell *The Lost One* many times to say *no,* but he continued to say *yes* again and again. Over time, we noticed he started to hang less and less with *us* and more and more with *them.*

One day, we pulled *The Lost One* to the side and asked him, "Why do you keep hanging out with *them?* They're going to get you locked up!"

The Lost One replied with a simple, "I don't know." But I think he really did know.

He didn't believe they were going to get caught. He even said it: "They never get caught." Two years later, he got caught.

The Lost One, the guy we had grown up with, was arrested for selling drugs and robbing a store. We hated to see this happen to our friend, but we'd be lying if we said we didn't see it coming.
What *The Lost One* got caught up in is what I see young leaders and students all around the country getting caught up in again and again. They believe

they're strong enough and smart enough to overcome the power of collective thought.

Collective thought means everybody's thinking the same thing, or thinking the same thing somebody else told them to be thinking.

Eventually, collective thought becomes a group's shared reality, whether it's *real* or not.

Collective thinking can cloud your decision making, but you don't even know it's confusing you because everybody else is thinking it too.

At the end of the day, what separates my friend who ended up in a leadership position at Google and my friend who wound up in jail was how they broke through that collective thinking and processed the decision to stay or go when *The Wrong Way* crowd started asking questions.

Even when everyone in your circle is thinking and doing the wrong thing, you somehow still think you'll be strong enough to do the right thing? Let me just go ahead and tell you the truth: This never works. Eventually, we all buckle under the pressure if we stick around long enough.

Our thoughts are usually not strong enough to overcome the collective thoughts of friends.

AND OUR THOUGHTS LEAD TO THE NEXT IMPORTANT PIECE OF THE PUZZLE: OUR DECISIONS.

I think we could apply *The Lost One's* story to this section as well. But let me tell you another one.

From eighth grade to eleventh grade, I went to a high school that specialized in a performing arts curriculum. One of the greatest things about attending a performing arts high school was the exposure it gave me to so many different avenues of artistic expression. The design of the school was to create an environment that was hyper-focused on developing our artistic talents. As you might imagine, it wasn't all classrooms and chalkboards. Every now and then, the teachers would take us out of class during the middle of the school day to attend a musical or a concert. Field trip!

They believed that if we could see something new—something designed, written, directed, produced, and performed at the highest skill level—it would help make us better artists. It would grow us, change us, and hopefully inspire us.

One day they took us to a musical called Soweto. It was about the policy of apartheid and separation in South Africa We were floored by this telling of the history of South African culture and the triumph of the people who lived in this township called Soweto on the outskirts of the capital city.

The musical took us onto the streets of South Africa and into a cultural revolution started by teenagers.

The songs were amazing, the harmonies were out of this world, and the acting was unbelievable. Some of the people from that musical went on to be on Broadway. As a student, it truly inspired me.

Watching these kids my age perform at the level they were performing at made me feel like I could be great like them. They looked like me. They dressed like me. They spoke like me. The only difference was they had found their voice and they were using it.

Something changed in me as I watched it, and I hoped

that one day I could be good enough to be part of a program like that. Now if I'm being honest, although my hope was deep, I still doubted that I could ever actually be that good.

After the show was over, a friend who was a little older than me pulled me to the side and spoke very strongly. He said, "One day, I want to see you on the stage with them. You have what it takes to do it. You should go talk to them today." In that moment, his words impacted me so much that my doubt instantly disappeared and I rushed to the dressing room and asked for the director of the theater company. He came out, and I pretty much yelled at him, "Sir! I have to be a part of what you guys are doing. I'll do anything!" He laughed at my excitement and invited me to come to their next rehearsal. I ended up in six shows with that company and went on to write more than ten original musicals with the director.

IT CHANGED MY LIFE FOREVER.

(That director's name was Freddie Hendricks. I just want to take a moment to thank him publicly for investing in me.)

How did I go from DOUBTING I'd ever be good enough to BOMBARDING the director backstage? The answer is my friend. He *changed* the way I saw myself and *influenced* me to change my decisions. It happened quickly. I had already determined that I wasn't ready to talk to anyone. I was going to walk right out of the theater with my doubt in hand. But my friend changed my decision with one sentence. It was almost as if his confidence was transferred into me with every word that he spoke.

> **Our decisions** *are* **highly influenced** *by the* **words** *and* **beliefs of our friends.**

AND LASTLY, LET'S TALK ABOUT ATMOSPHERE.

Growing up with other young artists and songwriters, we would often say, "The vibe is everything." I don't think we really knew what that meant. But we did know that sometimes writing songs was easier in creative, quiet spaces than loud, crazy spaces. In other words, the atmosphere could either help or hurt our ability to write. The atmosphere influenced the outcome.

Are you a writer? (Or a leader who writes?) Is it sometimes easier to write when you're alone?

Are you a student? When you're preparing for a test, are some environments better for studying than others?

Are you an athlete? Does going to a party the night before a big game affect your performance the next day?

I believe the same is true for success in life. If you're constantly in the wrong place, it doesn't matter how smart you are or how hard you try. *Being in the wrong atmosphere can consistently limit or even kill your success.*

I'll let you in on a secret I've learned: YOUR FRIENDS HELP CREATE SIXTY TO EIGHTY PERCENT OF

YOUR ATMOSPHERE.

Let me show you.

Growing up, my sister got straight A's. Like from Kindergarten all the way up to her senior year, she never got less than an A. It was insane. What's even more insane is that all of her friends got similar grades as well. As you can tell, that's not my story. I got all A's once! It was in my senior year . . . my last shot! Don't laugh. At least I tried! I usually landed somewhere around the B and maybe even C lane. And of course, you guessed it, so did my friends. One day, I asked myself why this was true. Why did all of my friends' grades mirror each other? What was the powerful force causing this?

Atmosphere.

I quickly realized we all rise to the level of excellence or mediocrity that is consistently around us. We hate to stand out. We hate to feel less than (or even greater than). There's something in all of us that wants to fit in somewhere. We want to be accepted in a group. And once we find ourselves in that group, we quickly become what the group requires. So we either push ourselves to be more, enhance where we already are, or dumb ourselves down to maintain the vibe of the group. Why? *Because we want to fit in.*

We become what the atmosphere demands of us—the atmosphere that's determined and created by our friends.

Our desire to fit in often outweighs our desire to stand out. Therefore, we become what the atmosphere of our friend group demands.

WHAT'S THE POINT?

I've spoken to more than a hundred thousand leaders and students over the past four years. Rich folk, poor folk, all races, and all belief systems. And the number one thing I've seen either helping or hurting every one of them? *Their circle of friends.*

I've seen privileged students destroy their lives hanging with the wrong crowd. I've seen students in underserved communities save their lives hanging with the right crowd. I've seen popular students leverage their influence to build up classmates everyone else overlooked. I've seen unpopular students teach popular students that there's more to life than just being the center of attention. They recognize that one day, when they enter a space where popularity doesn't matter, they should lean on things that do matter. Like valuing integrity and character over being cool.

My dream for every person reading this chapter is this:

That you will learn to take who your friends are seriously.

I hope you won't throw away such a powerful life lesson because you've heard it before, read it in a book, or because someone older than you said it. I hope you will receive it as truth and start building a better friend circle today. Why?

Because your friends will influence your thoughts which determine your decisions, ultimately creating your atmosphere. And I hope that atmosphere is filled with success rather than failure. Only you can determine that. But the good news is YOU HAVE THE CHOICE.

Find friends that make you better.

2 FIND YOUR VOICE

BY LISTENING TO WISE LEADERS

WHEN YOU GROW UP where I grew up and come from where I came from, everything in you wants to succeed. You *have* to succeed. My big dreams when I was young were to one day make it in the music industry or maybe even play professional basketball. As I watched people when I was growing up, they showed me that *in order to succeed, you have to find the right person to help you get there.* So my goal easily became: *Find a voice that can lead you to success.*

I quickly learned…

> ➤ That's harder than it sounds.
> ➤ Every leader isn't your leader.

The biggest lesson I learned from this was one I'll never forget:

NEVER FOLLOW SOMEONE THAT HASN'T BEEN WHERE YOU'RE TRYING TO GO.

You see, there was nothing wrong with my plan to find someone that could move me toward success. It just wasn't fully developed. Because while every person should find a leader who can help move them toward success, *not every leader should be followed.*

EVERY LEADER ISN'T RIGHT FOR EVERY PERSON.

By the end of this chapter, my goal is to show you a few things:

➢ Every person needs a chosen leader, somebody more than a friend, to guide them to success.
➢ Every leader isn't a leader you should be following.

> Choosing the wrong leader could lead you to failure instead of success.
> Every leader has a special gift to help someone succeed. You must find the leader that has the gifting you need.

We will discover these points by understanding how leaders influence our

thoughts,
decisions,
atmosphere,
and foresight.

Now I know what you're thinking: *"Haven't we already talked about the first three?"*

Yes, we have. But when it comes to leaders, they mean something a little different. They have an even more *profound* impact on your journey to success.

LET'S TALK ABOUT OUR THOUGHTS.

Believe it or not, your parents were (and possibly still are) leaders in your life. If you've never met your parents, then whoever raised you was your main leader growing up. I could tell you hundreds of stories about students who wouldn't give their very best in school or fight for more in life because of something their parents said to them when they were younger. For some, this type of verbal abuse or down-talking went on for years. I think some of you reading this can probably relate. They heard things like . . .

"You're not smart."
"You should be more like your brother."
"Wish you were more like your sister."
"How could you be so stupid?"
"You're worthless just like your daddy."
"I thought you'd grow up to be more."

Statements like this marked their childhoods and unfortunately determined how they saw themselves. It taught them what to think about who they were and the kind of potential they could have. When you hear negative statements like this from people who are leading you, those statements never leave you. It doesn't matter how old you are or how long it's been. It could be something your parents said or something your boss said or something your teacher said or even something your mentor or small group leader said. If it came from a leader in your life, it's very difficult to forget.

Your thoughts either rise or bow to the words your leaders spoke over you.

Here's how I know.

My adopted mom is amazing. She is truly one of the best moms you could ever imagine having. Growing up, she was supportive, nurturing, gracious, and truly inspirational.

But sometimes, she could be critical. Looking back, I don't think she actually knew she was tearing me down with her words. Sometimes she just did. For me and my twin sister, Sara, it was hard. I don't think my adopted mom wanted to be critical. I just think she didn't know how not to be. If you met my mom's mother, you would understand why my mom could be like that. My mom's mom also often expressed herself with words that were unkind and hurtful. I think it was their way of dealing with their own insecurities or low self-esteem. My mom never accomplished her childhood dreams. Instead, my sister and I became her dream. So I think she dealt with that lack of accomplishment in her own way with words like,

"That's not how the song goes."
"I'm not sure those lyrics make sense."
"That's not that good."

Sometimes when my dad would get angry, he'd jump in with his own commentary.

"That was a stupid thing to do."

Over the years, my mom and I have had many chances to talk about this, so it won't be a surprise to her when she reads this story in this book! She understands how I felt, where I was, and what I heard. We've both made changes along the way.

Listen to me. My parents were amazing. Both of them are truly incredible people. They literally changed my life. But like every parent, every human, they had their moments. Unfortunately, those moments affected me. When my mom would shoot down a song I'd been working on for days with a simple, "That's not good," I heard, "I'm not good." When my dad would get mad and say, "That was a stupid thing to do," I heard, "I'm stupid." Even though they'd say they never meant it that way, that's what I heard. So as a teenager, I struggled with confidence. I couldn't get past their words. I couldn't get past what my leaders spoke over me.

My guess is that some of you reading this can't get past some of the words your parents or leaders spoke over you. It's the reason you don't try harder. It's the reason you don't reach higher. It's the reason you don't run faster. You can't get past those words.

For me, it wasn't until a new leader entered my life and spoke new words over me that I was able to replace the old words holding me back. I needed a new leader to fight what the first leaders had put in my head. So if you're holding on to some words spoken over you in the past, allow me to be your new leader in this moment.

**Let it go.
Be Strong.
Your Life Matters.
You are Enough.
Go and Change
the World!**

Our thoughts about ourselves and our futures are heavily influenced by our leaders.

NOW LET'S TALK ABOUT OUR DECISIONS.

When I was 16 years old, I was offered my first record deal. I was so excited. I thought my dreams had come true. Then the CEO of the label put another leader in charge and said it would be that guy's job to make sure my album came out. This record executive was a rising star and I trusted the guy who had signed me, so it didn't matter to me who he wanted to put in charge of this deal. I was in no matter what. The CEO hadn't ever let me down or led me the wrong way, so I thought I could trust him.

I was patient as I waited for the album process to begin. After six months, nothing had happened. So I took it upon myself to let the CEO know that nothing was happening for our group. He told me not to worry, and to take all of my concerns to the leader he'd put in charge. I did just that.

I didn't have that person's phone number so I tracked him down one day walking through the halls of the organization. I approached him very nicely, "Hey sir, I haven't heard from you in six months. Are we still doing this album?" The leader looked at me and said, "Sorry bro, but I'm not concerned about you or your group. I have other artists and albums that I'm focused on. I won't be doing your album."

I was extremely upset. I stormed into the CEO's office and asked politely (or maybe I just thought it was polite) to speak with him about the label. His assistants once again told me to speak with the leader he had put in place. I insisted on speaking to the CEO, but he wouldn't see me. This process went on for nearly two years (insert shocked face here). I was so angry, sad, and upset. I had trusted both this CEO and the leader he'd put in place. I believed they would take care of me.

Unsure what to do next, I called a friend of mine and told him what happened. My friend told me to call another leader who worked in the music industry. By the time we met, I was basically crying from some combination of anger and sadness. I told him how I had put my life on hold for two years for this record executive who had promised he'd take care of me. I told him how his assistants kept putting me off. The new CEO looked me in the eye and said, "So all you've done for two years is ask nicely and wait?" I said, "Yes sir, I didn't want to make the CEO mad. I appreciate him for giving me a chance."

His response?

"Son, you've got to learn your own value. For him this is another business deal, but for you, this is your life. *Are you going to let him control your life or will you take the control back?*"

I was SO EMPOWERED by his words. The next day, I called the label office and told their team that I would need to explore my options for legal action if they didn't put my album out or release me from the contract. Within two minutes, the CEO called me directly and apologized for everything that had happened. He let me out of the deal without any issues. And that new CEO? Well, I let him lead me. I learned to trust him. With his guidance, I went on to have songs on the radio and to travel the world writing music with some of the biggest artists and producers in the industry.

What's the lesson here?

The right leader will lead us to success. The wrong leader will kill our success. Our decisions can lead to great success under the right leader.

NOW, ON TO ATMOSPHERE.

Marvin Gaye was one of the greatest musicians of all time. He was like the Justin Bieber or Drake of the 1960's. His songs reflected the time and challenged what was happening in one of the most pivotal decades in American history. One of his songs is called "What's Going On," and it talks about coming together as a people no matter what color you are. Or maybe you've heard the song, "Mercy, Mercy Me." Did you know that song is all about caring for the earth and the land that we've been given? It's a song about ecology! He was talking about climate change before climate change was cool (or warm, or whatever…that part's kind of confusing.) Anyway, Marvin Gaye is an American icon!

One day, a director came up to me and said, "I want you to play the piano and sing a full concert of Marvin Gaye's songs." I instantly thought this was a bad idea. I didn't think there was any way I was good enough to do this his iconic songs. But the director believed I was. When I assured him I was certainly not, he said, "Trust me." He told me he wanted me to put together a full set and to choose two or three musicians to play with me. That part I could do. I told him I had the perfect musicians already in mind to play with me, and I thought he'd be really excited. But he wasn't. He immediately looked right at me and said, "Those guys won't work. Those musicians are not as good as you are!"

"The reason you don't have freedom to be as good as you can be," he explained, "is because you keep playing with musicians who don't match your level of talent."

He told me if I wanted to become a better musician I needed to play with musicians who were better than me.

I doubted him. And I doubted him even more when he suggested that some of the best musicians in the country ought to play the concert with me. I doubted him because I was intimidated at the thought of playing with those guys. They were too good. I sure wasn't that good. Still, I trusted him. He encouraged me to try one rehearsal with them and to watch what the *atmosphere* might do for me.

So I did. As soon as the musicians walked in, I got nervous. These guys were big-time.

Again, the director told me to trust myself.
I began to tell these extraordinary musicians what to play and how my version of Marvin Gaye would go. As they started playing, it was as if they were in my head. Everything I had dreamed about the way the songs would sound happened when they played them. It was different with them. I sang differently. I took more risks. I got more creative. It was as if they were pulling things out of me that I didn't even know were there.

When I asked the director why he thought it was that I came alive with these musicians, he replied, "Because the atmosphere was right."

The atmosphere is about *energy.* The atmosphere is about creating a space for you to *be something.* That something can be better, mediocre, or even worse, but understand that the atmosphere creates the space for you to be something you haven't been yet. The musicians I played with before couldn't play what I needed them to play, the way I needed them to play it. Because of this, I had to play what they couldn't. This was keeping me from taking the songs to the next level. That director knew that by putting me with musicians who played with a greater excellence, I would be freed up to be more creative and comfortable. That, in turn, would allow for me to grow to another level. He helped me FIND MY VOICE.

Great leaders know when we're in the wrong atmosphere for success, and have the power to place us in the right one.

Now let's unpack how leaders influence our foresight.

WHAT IS FORESIGHT?

By definition, foresight is *the ability to predict what will happen or be needed in the future.*

That's not like having a crystal ball or some kind of magical power, but having the experience and insight to see where someone is headed because you can see where they are.

In other words, foresight is looking into the future and knowing what needs to happen for certain things to happen. In our case, that thing is success.

Don't miss this: Good leaders have great foresight.

Good leaders know how to look at where you are now and determine what you need to do today to be successful tomorrow. Atmosphere, decisions, thoughts—all of that is included in foresight. But what makes foresight different is that it requires more than those three things. Foresight is seeing beyond today's atmosphere, today's decisions, today's thoughts . . . to seeing what the future can be.

I've had leaders in my life with such foresight that they could meet me for the first time and tell me what I need to do next just by Googling my name. I've had leaders in my life look at me and tell me what I'm afraid of.

There's a statement that changes the game whenever you hear a leader say it. Get ready. Here it comes:

"You remind me of me."

Ooooooooooooooooooh, there it is!

What that good leader just said to you without saying it is this: "I've been where you are, and I know how to lead you to the next step." That leader is saying, "I know how to save you from the mistakes I've made." Great leaders have foresight partly because they've lived your life already. If you have a leader who hasn't been where you are trying to go…run! That leader will not help you get to the level of success you desire to get to because they don't understand where you're trying to go.

The right leader for you will be someone with the foresight to speed up your journey by saving you from unnecessary mistakes.

When I was 21, I moved back in with my parents. The music industry had changed and artists weren't making money from music anymore. You all know the story: The Internet created ways for anyone to download music for free, so record sales began to die. Everyone and their mother, big-name artists included, had to figure out how to make money again—including me.

I hated living at home. I was a grown man. The ladies weren't going to respect me at the crib with the parentals! So I tried to be gone from home as much as possible. I went to a friend's house in the rich part of town. He lived on the top floor overlooking the city. He was only 28 years old. I was awed and inspired every time I went over there.

One day, I just got fed up. I was done living at home and decided I had to put together a plan to move out… immediately. I had a couple of checks coming in from different gigs, so I had enough money to help me get started. My first plan was to live with my friend in his super -nice house and pay him a little rent. If that didn't work, I would find an affordable apartment.

When I approached my friend about moving in with him, he said something I'll never forget. It will stay with me forever: *"You have to make it rain. And once you make it rain, you have to keep it pouring."*

If you're wondering what he meant, don't worry, I did too!

He explained that he was once like me. He hated living at home. He saved enough money to move out and had the promise of some checks that were come in the future. After moving out on his own, he quickly realized that even though some of those checks were showing up, he did not really have enough money to consistently handle the true reality of living on his own.

So.

When his car needed work…and his computer broke…and his electricity bill skyrocketed…his paychecks were not enough to carry the extra expenses. They weren't consistent enough to pay his bills. He was all over the place. He hadn't asked anyone what to expect, and so he wasn't prepared for the extra bills.

He was making it rain, but he didn't have a system to keep it pouring.

He then asked me if I had more than enough or just enough. Of course, I only had just enough. I wasn't ready. I didn't have a system in place to keep it pouring—a steady paycheck coming at the same time every month. I was an artist. He knew what I didn't yet know: That no matter how much I wanted to, it wouldn't be wise for me to move out of my parents' house at that time.

He taught me this:

Great leaders have foresight that can save you from failure.

WHAT'S THE POINT?

Many people reject letting the right leader help them. A lot of them do this because the world makes us believe that if we admit we're weak, don't know something or need help, we're somehow not worthy. *Worthy of respect. Worthy of honor. Worthy of being taken seriously.* So we reject someone who can save us time, money, and failure just to prove that we're worthy to the world.

I'm not saying we shouldn't work hard to learn and discover as much as we can. I'm just saying that we all could be moving faster and learning more if we let great leaders help us as we grow.

After all, what you DO doesn't make you valuable. Who you ARE makes you valuable.

Are you a good person? Are you a hard worker? Are you generous? Can people trust you? Do you lift people up or tear them down? These are the qualities that make you valuable.

So my advice? Find your Leaders. Some of them are waiting on you. Coaches. Teachers. Millionaires. Pastors. Artists. Songwriters. Producers. Small group leaders. Parents. Mentors. They're out there!

> **BOTTOM LINE: Find LEADERS that make you GREATER**

3 FIND YOUR VOICE

BY RECOGNIZING YOUR FOLLOWERS

IN THE AGE OF SOCIAL MEDIA, having *followers* is a normal part of life. Whether we like it or not, we all have followers. Some of us may have six or seven, while others of us have thousands (depending on the platform you use).

The crazy thing about having followers today versus ten years ago is that, in the past, you had to earn your followers. You had to DO something that proved you should be followed. It's not really like that anymore. Now, we can gain followers pretty easily. If someone knows us, likes our pictures, or loves our status, they will follow us.

The good thing about that is that we all have the chance to influence people without having to do much to earn it. But the bad thing about that is that we all have the chance to influence people without having to do much to earn it!

In order to make the best of our influence and the followers we have, I think we need to stop and ask ourselves the following questions:

Who is following me?
Why are they following me?
Who am I leading?
Why am I leading them?
How will I use my influence to make a difference?

Before we dive into those, let me tell you a story.

There was a boy who grew up in Memphis, Tennessee. He loved Elvis Presley's music and jumping off of houses. He was addicted to wonder and discovery; passion motivated his every move. As that little boy grew older, he started noticing other little boys and girls just like him. He noticed other kids that loved living life the same way he did. No worries, no cares . . . just life. He wanted to do everything he could to create a world that would never take that spirit, feeling, or life away from them.

And he did just that. He hosted sleepovers, hangouts, and moments where kids just like him could let their imaginations come to life. I don't know if he knew he was really doing it at the time. I think he was just being himself and it sort of just happened.

As that boy grew up and became a man, he saw something else. He started to see that there were kids from all over the country who wanted to live life the way he did as a kid. But for one reason or another, they couldn't. Maybe their parents didn't have the money. Or their parents couldn't take care of them and gave them away. Or maybe they had people in their lives that threatened to steal that life from them. Whatever their situations were, they kept them from having what that man wanted them to have—the same kind of childhood he had as a boy (or even greater).

So what did he do? Well, the man decided to start a movement that worked with churches, schools, parents, and students to give them that kind of life. He believed that every kid deserves to have great friends, make wise choices, and experience true faith. He believed that every kid deserves to live life to the full.

What's special about this story is that without that little boy, this book would not exist. Why? Because I met that little kid as a man, and he told me to write this book for everyone around the world who dreams of a better future. He told me to write it because he wanted to be a part of launching this message to the world.

The reason I tell you this story is because when kids, students, and leaders decide to take their current and future followers seriously, they have the potential to change the world for the better. They can do big things. They can start major movements. They can change lives. They can become heroes.

My hope is that as we unpack the five questions listed above, you will be inspired to use the voice that's screaming loudly on the inside of you.

WHO IS FOLLOWING YOU?

We've been talking about the influence that friends and leaders have on you—how their influence can cause you to either succeed or fail. Well, the same is true about you. You're someone's friend or leader. There are people following you right now that you have no idea about. There are probably some you haven't even met. That's why when it comes to using your influence well, it's important to start by discovering who your followers really are.

I'm not talking about their names. I'm talking about their identities.

Where did they grow up?
What do they like?
What are their dreams?
What are their passions?
What are their gifts and talents?
What makes them, them? Who are they?

KNOWING WHO YOUR FOLLOWERS ARE helps you understand the opportunity in front of you. Knowing who they are teaches you about you. Knowing who's following you says something about the way you were created.

When I learn about the people who have been influenced by me, it humbles me, it encourages me, and it inspires me. But most importantly, it teaches me what I need to become better at to be a better leader. What opportunities do I have to help somebody and what do I need to get better at in order to do it?

A young leader once asked me for a one-on-one meeting. He said he'd been watching me speak to adults and students over the years and had built his entire style of communication by watching me communicate. I was shocked. He told me that he was from a small town and was trying to figure out how to make it as a young black leader in a culture that has more than just black people in it.

A couple of things happened after he shared that with me. I immediately thought to myself, *I need to make more time in my life to help guys like him. I need to do more one-on-one meetings. In those meetings, I need to share more about how I've been able to do what this guy is telling me he's trying to do right now.*

Learning about someone who was following me taught me how I could be better in leading and helping them.

WHY ARE THEY FOLLOWING YOU?

A mentor once told me to always check a person's motives. Not everyone who comes around is following you for the right reasons. Some people follow you with the hopes of being inspired, of course. But others follow to stay close with the hopes of defeating you, stopping you, or even taking advantage of you. Regardless of their motive for following you, the best decision you can ever make as a leader is to find out why the people who follow you are actually following you.

Why do people follow you on social media?
Why do people follow you in life?
What's their goal?
What do they see in you that makes them want to follow you?
What is it about you that people see and want to be?

In 2018, Marvel Comics released Black Panther, a movie that broke records, united races, and tore down barriers. You may have seen it (I saw it five times). I love this movie partially because I'm African-American (black), but also because it was cool to see an entire country display such bravery.

There's a scene in the movie where T'Challa (a.k.a. the Black Panther) is stripped of his power as he's getting ready to be crowned king. In the culture of Wakanda (the nation where the film takes place), before T'Challa could take the throne, he had to battle any other warriors who wanted to challenge his place as king. In order to make the fight fair, he had to give up the special powers he had as the Black Panther. In a surprise move, the King of the Jabari mountain tribe steps up to challenge T'Challa for the throne. This guy is big, strong, and angry. When M'baku fights T'Challa, he fights with everything in him.

After a back-and-forth battle, M'Baku sneaks in what seems to be the unexpected and fatal blow. It's apparent to everyone that T'Challa is going to lose. He is bleeding, out of energy, and out of time.

But then T'Challa hears his mother yell out, "Show him who you are!"

Her words cause T'Challa to jump out of his defeat and head-butt his opponent. The chance to defeat and kill

M'baku is right in his hands. But T'Challa pauses. He tells his opponent, "Tap out! I don't want to kill you! Your tribe needs you." And M'baku listens. He taps out, and T'Challa becomes king of all tribes in Wakanda. In that moment, all committed to following King T'Challa until his dying breath.

The tribes followed King T'Challa because he *fought well, showed bravery,* and *proved that he was merciful.* Those specific things made him a leader that people wanted to follow.

And the same could be true of you. What are those things that are special about you? What qualities do you have that make people want to follow you?

When you discover why people are following you, you'll discover your true hidden power.

WHO ARE YOU LEADING?

A leadership coach once asked this question: *"How do you know you're a leader? You turn around and see if anyone is following you."* I love his answer. There may be many people following us. But I think the important question to ask is this: Are the people following us going where we want them to go?

Do we care where they go or what they do?
Have we decided to really take them somewhere?
Are we actually leading? Or are we just living?

For years, the greatest problem America has had with celebrities is that they gain millions of followers through popularity but never accept the responsibility that comes with actually leading those followers. In other words, they become leaders with no plan to truly lead.

My friends, this is the problem with our world today. There are so many people (even students!) gaining hundreds, thousands, and millions of followers. But they don't realize the *magnitude* of their influence and don't want to accept the responsibility of leading.

Our world has taught us that our popularity comes without responsibility. I think we all want to believe that, because it makes having power a lot easier. It gives us power without sacrifice. I mean, wouldn't life be great if we could only eat sweets and never have to touch a vegetable? Or play sports without stretching? Or have strength without ever having to work out? We all know life doesn't work that way. We can't have one without the other. And leadership and influence work the same way.

You can't have a bunch of followers without taking responsibility for how you lead them.

We've grown up in a generation that believes having followers doesn't necessarily mean we're leaders. But I'm here to tell you that, in fact, it does. It really does. If you have followers, you're a leader.

So I'll ask you this another way: *Are you thinking about where you're leading the people who are following you? Or are you just thinking about yourself?*

When we think about where we're leading the people following us, we become leaders worth following.

WHY ARE YOU LEADING THEM?

In the last section, we came to the conclusion that we need to take the people who are following us seriously. We talked about the way in which celebrities gain influence and popularity without wanting to take responsibility for the people who are following them. And we encouraged you to take responsibility for your own influence and followers.

While all of that is great, it's only a first step. The next step should be deciding on your special why for leading. It's great to care about your followers and pay attention to where you're taking them, but you can't stop there. You must decide why you care. I know it may sound like I'm repeating myself here, but I promise, I'm not.

Just "follow" me for a sec! *(See what I did there? #joke)*

In the movie *The Greatest Showman,* we see the story of how P.T. Barnum created an amazing version of what we now call the circus. Back then, he started the circus for a few reasons.

He needed to feed his family.
He wanted to make a name for himself.
He wanted to create a space for outcasts to be celebrated.

From the outside looking in, it was a great idea. But in order for him to accomplish his third goal, he had to convince dozens of people who were seen as outcasts in their world to follow him into this crazy new thing called the circus.

As we all know, he did it. But how? In the movie, he did it by telling them that never again would people laugh at them for being different. He told them that the circus would be the one place where their differences wouldn't separate them from others. He told them that the circus would be their home. His deep (and unique) *why* was creating a home for these people.

To make a long story short, P.T. Barnum got lost in success as the circus exploded. He started to care more about his first two *whys* and less about his deep *why*— the why he used to recruit his entire team. He started to chase more and more success, only to eventually lose everything that mattered.

Along the way, he traded the outcasts for the in-crowd. He traded an oasis of acceptance for a shallow life of being well-known. In the end, he eventually lost the fame, fortune, and followers of the in-crowd. The most extraordinary thing about the end of this story is that the outcasts were the ones who returned to him and stood by his side.

In that moment, he learned a very valuable lesson: Anytime you trade your deep *why* for a shallow *why,* you lose your way.

The point of me telling you this story is to draw a picture for you of what it looks like for a person to have multiple *whys.* It's to help you understand that you can sometimes choose the wrong *why* on your list. It is so important that you take time to decide on your deep *why.* Don't just assume you have the right one simply because you chose to care about your followers.

Take time to really think and choose the right *why*. P.T. Barnum got lost chasing the wrong *why*—success. He traded his deep and meaningful *why* for a shallow and selfish one. In doing so, he left the people he'd convinced to follow him without the home he promised them.

Choosing the right *why* makes it difficult to lose your way with your followers.

HOW WILL YOU USE YOUR INFLUENCE TO MAKE A DIFFERENCE?

So what are you going to do?

I think we've discovered together what we should do, but *what are actually going to do?*

The good thing about gaining followers so easily in this age of social media is that we can make a big difference very quickly. There are so many problems in the world. There are so many people who need someone to lead them toward a better life.

> **BOTTOM LINE: Find FOLLOWERS that you can lead to purpose.**

IT'S TIME TO FIND YOUR VOICE

We all remember that friend, small group leader, mentor, parent, or neighbor who cared enough about us to tell us the truth. They cared enough to help us. They cared enough to lead us. Isn't that what leadership and influence is all about? Helping people?

That's why you should FIND YOUR VOICE.

You should FIND YOUR VOICE and raise it because people need help.

You should FIND YOUR VOICE and raise it to make a difference.

You should FIND YOUR VOICE and raise it to discover your greatness.

That's what this life is all about—using the years we've been given to help someone or something get better. Imagine a world filled with people who have made the decision to lead everyone that follows them in life and online to a better place.

That would be a world that everyone would want to live in. It would be a world full of greatness, created and led by people who understand the power of influence—*people who have found their voices.*